A Sense
of the Ridicu

A Play

Rae Terence

Samuel French – London
New York – Sydney – Toronto – Hollywood

Please note our NEW ADDRESS:

Samuel French Ltd

52 Fitzroy Street London W1P 6JR

Tel: 01 - 387 9373

CHARACTERS

Mary
Mother
Uncle Henry
Body

The action takes place in the lounge of a large, suburban house.

Time—the present

A SENSE OF THE RIDICULOUS

The lounge of a large suburban house

There is a door to the hall UL, *a fireplace* DL *and french windows in the rear wall* R. *The furniture, which has an air of faded gentility, consists of a dining-table* L *against the rear wall, with a chair at each end, an armchair* C *and a settee* R, *set at an angle. Downstage of the settee is a small table with a telephone and an envelope on it*

When the CURTAIN *rises the door* UL *is ajar, so that it masks the dining-table, on which lies the body of a man of indeterminate age; his feet towards the door, his arms folded across his chest and a bowler hat on his stomach. The stage is in darkness except for a single spot on the pale face of the Body*

The Lights come up to full as Mary *is heard off*

Mary (*off*) Mother, I'm home.

The telephone starts to ring

> *Mary enters from the hall, carrying a small case and a handbag. She is thirty, and wears a light summer dress and white gloves. She puts the case and handbag on the armchair and removes her gloves. Then she goes and sits on the settee and answers the telephone*

Hello. Three–two–six–two. . . . Paul! How nice to hear from you. . . . Yes, I've been in London for a couple of days. Just this second got back. . . . No. Strictly pleasure. I went to visit a friend who I was at Medical School with. . . . (*She laughs*) *She* has a husband and three kids. . . . I'd love to go. . . . Half-past seven would be fine. . . . (*She laughs*) Oh! I'll have to see how I feel tonight before I agree to that. . . . (*She laughs*) I'll see *you* later. Bye! (*She puts down the telephone and stands up. She picks up the envelope and looks at the writing. She turns to face unstage*) Mother, I'm . . . (*She sees the Body and gives a cry of anguish*) Oh no . . . not another one! (*She moves to the table, lifts the Body's left arm and tests for a pulse. After a few seconds she releases the arm, which falls limply on to the chest of the Body*) Really this is too much! (*She marches to the door; shouting*) Mother, will you come into the lounge please!

Mother (*off*) I'll be there in a minute, dear. I'm just finishing ...

Mary I don't care what you are doing, please come in here now! (*Mary moves to the table and stands there, impatiently tapping the envelope against her hand*)

Mother enters. She is in her sixties, and is wiping her hands on her apron

Mother Now then, dear, I can't stay long because I'm in the middle of baking. Did you enjoy yourself in London? I hope the journey home hasn't given you a headache and made you cross. You know, even as a child you were never a good traveller. I can remember a time when——

Mary (*interrupting*) Mother, I have not got a headache, but I am very cross. (*Pointing to the Body*) What is this?

Mother (*after a pause*) It looks like a dead body, dear.

Mary I know it's a dead body. What is it doing here? I thought we'd agreed after the last one that ...

Mother Oh it isn't one of mine, dear.

Mary I beg your pardon?

Mother I said it isn't one of mine.

Mary Are you sure?

Henry is seen peering in through the french windows

Mother Well, of course I am, dear. I mean, just look at it. Does it look like one of mine?

Mary Now you mention it ... (*She sees Henry at the window*) Uncle Henry!

Henry moves quickly out of sight

Mary exits quickly by the hall door

Mother examines the Body

Mother (*going and sitting on the end of the settee*) Fancy her thinking it's one of mine.

Mary (*off*) Uncle Henry, will you come in the lounge, please. Now don't argue, just come in.

Mary enters, followed by Henry. He is in his sixties, and carries a small axe

Henry Now what is it? I've got a lot of work to do in the garden and I haven't time to be chatting.

Mother I see you've been pruning the roses.

Henry You don't prune roses with an axe, you fool.

Mother You do surprise me. Last time you pruned them they looked just as though you'd used an axe.

Henry What would you know about it? As far as you're aware——

Mary Mother! Uncle Henry! Stop it! Save your silly argument for later. Now then, Uncle Henry, what is that Body doing there?

Henry (*after a pause*) Lying in state?

Mother bursts out laughing

Mary (*exasperatedly*) Uncle Henry, do try and be serious!

Henry Well, how should I know what it's doing there? Why don't you ask giggling Gertie there?

Mother It isn't mine!

Henry It must be.

Mary All right! All right! This has gone far enough. (*She goes to the armchair and picks up the case and handbag*) Uncle Henry, come and sit down here.

Henry sits in the armchair. Mary places the case and handbag on the floor at the upstage end of the settee and then stands between the armchair and the settee

Now, listen very carefully, both of you. It's going to be very difficult to get rid of this one, now that we haven't got the car. You both promised that there wouldn't be any more and one of you has broken that promise. Now then, I want the truth. Mother?

Mother I don't know how you can suggest that I am not telling the truth. I'm only glad that your father isn't here to witness it.

Henry Well I hope you're not suggesting that I'm lying, because let me tell you, young lady, that in my day we were taught to speak the truth and shame the devil.

Mary (*shouting*) Well one of you must be lying!

The Body suddenly sits up on the table. He is of indeterminate age. He has a pleasant, easy manner but there is something sinister about him

Body (*with an Irish accent*) Here! Here! Here! What's all this shouting? Can you not let a body sleep in peace?

The effect is electric. Mother screams and falls back on the settee. Henry shouts "Oh my God", *clutches his heart, and falls back in the armchair. Mary swings round open-mouthed, and drops the envelope on the floor. Body jumps off the table, retrieves the letter and hands it to Mary*

You dropped your letter. (*Putting on the bowler hat*) You don't mind if I wear me hat, do you? It's just that I feel half naked without it.

Mary (*taking the letter; stammering*) B—but ... you're dead!

Body (*indignantly*) I'm not!

Mother I wouldn't argue with her, she's a doctor you know.

Body (*moving away* DL) Is that a fact? Well, ordinarily I wouldn't dream of questioning the judgement of a doctor, but I do think if a man is dead then he's probably the first to know about it.

Mary What are you doing here?

Body Until a few minutes ago I was sleeping peacefully. (*To Henry*) You know it could be fatal to a man being woken up like that.

Henry Sorry about that, old boy, wasn't thinking.

Mary Don't apologize to him! He's broken in, stolen God knows what ...

Body Here! Here! That's a bit strong. I haven't broken into anywhere, and I can't have stolen anything because I'm still here.

Mother He's quite right you know, dear.

Mary Shut up, Mother.

Body Is that any way for a girl to be speaking to her mother? (*To Mother*) Missus, you remind me of my own dear mother, rest her soul. I would never have spoken to her in such a fashion. (*To Henry*) She'd have split me gob if I had done.

Mary You can stop all that blarney right now. Where do you come from and how did you get in?

Body As to where I come from, that must have been obvious the moment I opened me mouth. But to answer the second part of the question. Yesterday evening, as I strolled down the road on my way from there to here, I was overcome by the sheer beauty of the display of roses in your front garden. (*To Henry*) I put it down to skilful pruning myself.

Henry (*to Mother*) There you are. What did I tell you?

Body Anyway, I felt that I just had to congratulate whoever was responsible. There was nobody at the front of the house, so I walked round the back, and do you know I couldn't find anyone there either, but I did find the french windows wide open. Well, that didn't seem quite right, I mean, there are lots of dishonest folk about, so I decided to wait and guard the premises until the owners returned. I suppose I must have fallen asleep on the job.

Mary (*going to the fireplace and putting the envelope on the mantelshelf*) How did you say you got into the house?

Body Through the french windows. Of course, I closed them when I came in.

Mary And the windows were open you say?

Body Wide open. (*Grasping his lapels*) The case for the defence rests.

Mary That is your first and last mistake. Those windows have not been opened for over three years, and do you know why? Because Uncle Henry lost the keys!

Henry She's got a good point there, old boy. Difficult to counter that.

Body (*deliberately*) They were open last night!

Mary I'll damn well prove it to you. (*She moves quickly to the windows and grasps the handles*) Look! (*To her great surprise the windows open easily*)

Body (*quietly*) Look indeed.

Mary Uncle Henry?

Henry Nothing to do with me.

Mother And it's nothing to do with me either. Well, now we've sorted that out why don't we all sit down, and I'll make a pot of tea?

Body Missus, you've been reading my mind. I was only just thinking to myself ...

Mary (*picking up the case and handbag*) I am taking these upstairs. When I come down I expect to find you gone. If you are still here I shall call the police.

She sweeps out of the hall door

Body Ahem. I get the impression that she doesn't really approve of me.

Henry I shouldn't let it worry you, old boy, she doesn't really approve of anybody very much. Well, you'd better be on your way. She'll be down in a minute. (*He stands up, puts the axe on the dining-table, and goes to the window*) I'll let you out this way. (*He tries to open the window but it is locked*) Bless my soul! Damn thing seems to have locked itself. (*He tries the window again without success*) Most peculiar.

Body Ah, don't worry about it, I was thinking of staying for a little while longer anyway. (*He sits in the armchair*)

Henry You please yourself of course, but she means it y'know, she will call the police.

Mother I don't know why she wants to make all this fuss. There's been no harm done, and I find it very pleasant to talk to somebody different.

Body Missus, as soon as I set eyes on you I said to myself, there is a charming lady.

Mother (*embarrassed but pleased*) Oh really!

Body And it's easy to see where your daughter's good looks come from.

Mother Oh really!

Body Er, did you mention something about a cup of tea? It's very thirsty work, this guarding of premises, y'know.

Mother Oh, of course. What must you think of me? (*She goes to the door*) Do you want some tea, Henry?

Henry I might as well. I'm staying to see the fun when Mary comes down anyway. (*He pulls out a chair at the dining-table* R *and sits on it*)

Mother I won't be long. (*She turns to go*)

Mary enters

Mary Where are you going, Mother?

Mother Just to make some tea for our guest.

Mary There's no need.

Mother But ...

Mary (*moving to the armchair*) I said there's no need! Our guest isn't stopping!

Body Well, I'm not thinking of departing just yet.

Mary In that case you leave me with no alternative but to call the police. (*She goes to the telephone*)

Body I don't think that would be wise, in view of the circumstances.

They all freeze, then turn to look at him

Henry Circumstances, old boy. What do you mean, circumstances?

Body (*easily*) Well I mean. What could they do? No crime has been committed. Has it?

Mary What about trespass?

Body Trespass is a civil offence, not criminal. Because it might be — embarrassing for you to have the police call here.

After a pause Mary comes to a decision

Mary Mother, why don't you fetch our guest one or two of your buttered scones?

Mother (*surprised*) Do you think I should?

Mary Yes I do. We must try to be hospitable. Oh, and Uncle Henry, why don't you fetch a bottle of your elderberry wine? (*To Body*) Uncle Henry's wines are quite exceptional.

Body Elderberry wine is a particular favourite of mine. Would it be possible at all for me to wash my hands?

Mary The bathroom is the first door at the top of the stairs.

Body (*standing*) Thank you. (*He goes to the door, then turns; to Mother*) Two scones will be ample for me.

He exits

Pause. Mother goes to the door

Mother (*returning*) Mary, do we have to give him some scones?

Mary Yes, Mother, we do. There's something about him that worries me.

Mother Oh, what a pity. I rather like him.

Mary Come on, Uncle Henry. Fetch a bottle of wine.

Henry (*doubtfully*) I don't know as we should.

Mary Why not?

Henry Well, it doesn't seem right. (*To Mother*) What do you think?

Mother I'm not very keen. It seems ... unnecessary.

Mary Unnecessary! There's something very odd about him. I think he knows — and if he does, he's a danger to us all.

Henry We don't know that he knows. The trouble with you, Mary, is that you're too suspicious.

Mother It would be a shame if ...

Mary Don't tell me you two are getting squeamish. What is it now? Twenty-three?

Henry Twenty-two! We don't count the vicar.

Mary I think the police would. Now, no more arguments. Fetch in the scones and the wine.

Henry If you say so, m'dear. Seems a damn shame though.

Henry and Mother exit

Mary moves nervously round the room and finishes DL

The Body enters

Body I feel all the better for that. (*Approaching Mary*) Can I ask why you changed your mind?

Mary (*coldly*) I have not changed my mind. You are leaving this house today ... one way or another. I merely thought that something to eat might help you on your way.

Body (*sitting in the armchair*) Ah, you don't fool me one little bit. Beneath that hard exterior you're a very nice person ... and admit it now, you really find me quite attractive, don't you?

Mary (*furiously*) You are bloody insufferable!

Mother and Henry enter. Mother carries a plate with two scones. Henry carries a bottle and a glass

Mother (*gaily*) Here we are then, a special treat for a special guest. (*She puts the plate on Body's knee, and sits on the settee*)

Henry pours a glass of wine. He places the bottle on the table, and hands the glass to Body. He then sits on the settee. Mother and Henry watch Body eagerly

Body (*indicating the scones*) Will you just look at them. You know, a man could die just by contemplating such perfection. (*He sniffs the wine; to Henry*) You rascal you. I can tell this is a really powerful vintage. (*He lifts a scone to his mouth*)

They all lean forward

(*Lowering the scone*) Is nobody going to join me in some refreshment?

Mary We've all had breakfast.

Body So you have. So you have. (*He lifts the scone*)

They all lean forward

(*Lowering it again; to Mother*) Excuse me for asking, but this is real butter, isn't it? I don't like to appear rude, but I'm allergic to margarine. It brings me out in a rash.

Mother Oh yes! Yes! I never use anything else.

Body That's all right then. (*He quickly devours the scone in two bites, drinks half the wine and smacks his lips*)

Mother clasps her hands and gives a little moan. Henry sighs. They both relax and lean back

I'm really on a diet, but that scone was so delicious it would be a sin not to have the other. (*He devours the other scone, drinks the remainder of the wine and then leans back in the chair*)

Henry stands, takes the plate and glass, and places them on the table, then stands behind the armchair. There is a pause. Mother looks at Henry, who shrugs

Henry Ahem. D'you feel all right, old boy?

Body Y'know, it's funny you should ask that, but I was only just thinking that I never felt better.

Mary and Mother exchange puzzled glances

Mother Was everything to your satisfaction?

Body (*beaming*) It's only my opinion of course, and I don't claim to be an expert, but I think there was just a little too much strychnine in the wine. But the ground glass in the scones was done to perfection.

Mother screams and falls back. Henry grabs the axe from the dining-table and lifts it above his head as though to strike the Body. Mary watches, thunderstruck. The Body remains smilingly unconcerned. The tableau is held in silence, then Henry slowly lowers the axe and sits on the settee. Mother and Henry remain still, staring straight ahead

There, that's a lot more friendly, isn't it? You know, Henry, violent exercise at your age could be dangerous. Besides which you would have damaged me hat!

Mary Who are you?

Body (*standing*) That all depends on where in the world you happen to live.

Mary I don't understand.

Body (*to Mother*) Missus, why don't you and your brother take the
things back into the kitchen?

*Mother and Henry stand; she takes the plate, he puts the axe on the
table and takes the bottle and glass. They exit*

(*Gently*) Now then, Mary, sit yourself down.

She sits in the armchair

There, that's better. (*He lies back on the settee*) You ask who I
am. The Ancient Greeks used to call me Pan, in India I am known
as Shiva. In this part of the world I am known by several names:
Lucifer, Satan—I prefer Old Nick myself.

Mary The Devil?

Body Himself.

Mary Don't be ridiculous!

Body And what's ridiculous about it?

Mary Well. Whoever heard of the Devil with an Irish accent?

Body (*laughing*) I'll grant you that if I turned up in Outer Mongolia
with an Irish accent, it would tend to confuse the native
population, but round here, well, why not? Anyway I like the
Irish. They have a wonderful sense of the ridiculous.

Mary You're mad! I'm not staying here to listen to any more of this
rubbish. (*She stands and makes for the door, but instead circles the
armchair and finishes by the settee, very bewildered*)

Body (*gently*) It doesn't matter which direction you run, Mary,
you'll always end up face to face with me.

Mary covers her face with her hands

There! There! Sit down again and don't upset yourself.

Mary (*sitting*) I'm frightened.

Body I haven't done anything so terrible have I?

Mary But you're supposed to be evil.

Body You mustn't believe everything you read in the bible, Mary.
(*Smiling*) After all, it's very biased where I'm concerned.

Mary Why have you come here? What do you want?

Body (*sighing*) Well, I've come for those two old reprobates in the
kitchen.

Mary (*wailing*) No!

Body I'm afraid so.

Mary But, they're just like innocent children.

Body (*rising and moving* DL; *impatiently*) Innocent are they! Mother of God!

Black-out. There is a flash of lightning and a clap of thunder. The Lights come up again

(*Calmly*) All right! All right! I'm sorry. He's getting very touchy, you know. How can you say they're innocent when they've murdered twenty-three people?

Mary Twenty-two. The vicar was a mistake — by Uncle Henry. They don't really mean any harm, and the thought of you sending them to hell is just too horrible.

Body Now just hold on a minute. I don't send anyone to hell. (*Pointing upwards*) He sends people to hell! I just try to accommodate them. And I don't mind telling you it's getting pretty full. (*Looking upwards*) I'm thinking of putting up a sign, "No room at the Inn".

There is a dull rumble of thunder

Aye, well, you just think about it.

Mary But the thought of them suffering for all eternity …

Body Hell isn't so bad, once you get used to it. And as for suffering, don't forget I've been there longer than anyone.

Mary What sort of a place is it?

Body (*to himself*) Hell isn't a place, it's a state of mind. Each individual's hell is personal, and different.

Mary Why are you telling me all this?

Body Ah yes. Well, you see, before anyone goes to hell they have to be told, and they have to be told why. (*Pointing upwards*) That's another of the rules. It's not something I relish, meself. I just thought it might come easier from yourself.

Mary Oh no! I couldn't. (*Pleading*) I couldn't!

Body You could tell them you'll be joining them yourself before very long.

Mary shakes her head in horror

Well please yourself, but time is passing, and I can delay no longer.

Mother and Henry enter

Henry And that's why the colonel's daughter couldn't find her knickers.

Mother (*chuckling*) Henry, that story changes every time I hear it. (*She sits on the settee*)

Henry stands behind the armchair

Well now. Have you two been having a nice chat?

Body (*sadly*) That we have, missus, that we have. I think Mary has something to tell you. (*He turns away*)

Mary This gentleman, er, isn't really a—a gentleman at all. In fact he's—he's ... (*She looks round helplessly*)

Mother Go on, dear.

Mary It sounds so silly, but well, he's the Devil.

Henry and Mother show no surprise

Mother (*calmly*) Yes, dear.

Mary And he's—he's come to take you with him. (*She covers her face with her hands and starts to sob*)

Mother I see.

Henry D'you mean take us down to—down to—er ...

Body Aye.

Henry Are we allowed to ask why?

Body Oh yes. (*Glancing upwards*) All the formalities have to be completed. For the murder of twenty-two persons, plus the vicar who was a mistake.

Mother Oh, don't say murder.

Body Well, what would you call it?

Mother We just thought that they must be unhappy with the wicked lives they were leading. We looked on it more as putting them to rest.

Body Putting them to rest! (*He laughs*) Aren't all twenty-three with me at this very moment? And getting precious little rest, I can tell you.

Henry All twenty-three?

Mother (*shocked*) Not the vicar too!

Body He was that twisted he could hide behind a spiral staircase.

Henry I find that difficult to believe.

Body What do you think he was doing in the nunnery gardens at two o'clock in the morning?

Henry I did wonder about that.

Body Peeping, that's what he was doing. Peeping!

Henry Bless my soul!

Body That's enough of that kind of talk! Come on now, it's time we were on our way.

Mother (*standing*) Will it take long to get there?

Body No. Hell isn't far away. (*Looking at Mary*) For some people it's here already.

Mother and Henry exit

(*After a pause*) Thank you for your help, Mary. I know it wasn't easy. (*He takes the envelope from the mantelshelf and hands it to her*) You can read your letter in peace now.

Mary I'm going to be awfully lonely without them.

Body Nonsense. You don't need them. A young woman like you, living in a fine house like this, what a time you could have. You don't need them.

Mary (*standing*) Why don't you take me as well?

Body (*pointing upwards*) You'll have to ask Him that. I only obey orders. And anyway, I'll have me hands full for a while with those two. But I'll be back, don't you worry, I'll be back. Goodbye, Mary. (*He goes to the door, then turns*) Don't forget, you don't need them.

He exits, closing the door behind him

Mary stands motionless for a moment. The door bursts open, startling her

Mother enters. She is wearing a coat and carrying two heavy shopping bags. She is altogether a much coarser woman than the one who left earlier

Mother That bloody walk from the shops seems to get longer every time. Why your father had to buy a house at the top of a bloody hill, I never did understand.

Mary The view.

Mother What?

Mary I said the view. He probably bought it for the view.

Mother Fat lot of good it did him. Eight months after we moved he dropped dead. Probably the strain of walking up that bloody hill. (*Angrily*) It didn't used to be so bad when you had a car.

Mary I can't afford a car until I can get a job.

Mother Well, don't you think you should be trying to get one?

Mary You know the doctors said I had to rest.

Mother There's a difference between resting and being bone idle. I don't suppose you've done anything to the house. Have you cleaned up the kitchen?

Mary No — I'll — I'll do it now.

Mother Don't bother, I'll do it. I'll do it all. Why should today be any different? Where's your Uncle Henry?

Mary He's still in bed, I think.

Mother Trying to sleep off last night's binge, I suppose. I've just about had enough. What with a brother who's a permanent drunk, and a daughter who's a nutcase.

Mary You shouldn't say that about me!

Mother Why not? It's the truth. You've been locked away twice.

Mary I've been in hospital!

Mother You can call it that if you want. All I know is that it had bars on the windows.

Mother exits

Mary It couldn't have been a dream. It was too real. He was here. I know he was!

Mother (*off; shouting*) Henry, get out of bed and don't come down till you've cleaned yourself up.

Mary picks up the axe from the table. During the following speech the stage gradually darkens

Mary What was it he said? You don't need them. Yes, that was it. Young woman like you ... fine house ... You don't need them!

Mary exits

Black-out. We hear a short, loud scream, off, from Mother, followed immediately by a flash of lightning, and a crash of thunder

In the lightning, the figure of a man in a bowler hat is seen at the french windows

CURTAIN

FURNITURE AND PROPERTY LIST

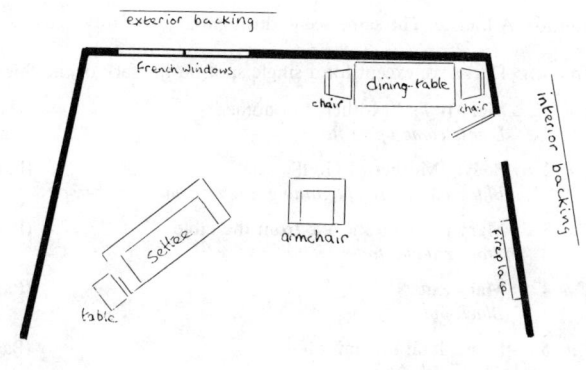

On stage: Armchair
Settee
Small table. *On it:* telephone, envelope
Dining-table
2 dining chairs

Off stage: Small case, handbag **(Mary)**
Small axe **(Henry)**
Plate with 2 scones **(Mother)**
Bottle of wine, wine glass **(Henry)**
2 full shopping bags **(Mother)**

LIGHTING PLOT

Property fittings required: nil

Interior. A lounge. The same scene throughout

To open: Darkness, except for a single spot on the face of the **Body**

Cue 1	**Mary** (*off*): "Mother, I'm home." *Lights come up to full*	(Page 1)
Cue 2	**Body:** "Mother of God!" *Black-out. Flash of lightning. Lights come up as before*	(Page 11)
Cue 3	**Mary** picks up the axe from the table *Start gradual fade*	(Page 14)
Cue 4	**Mary** exits *Black-out*	(Page 14)
Cue 5	Short, loud scream, off *Flash of lightning*	(Page 14)

EFFECTS PLOT

Cue 1   **Mary** (*off*): "Mother, I'm home."   (Page 1)
         Telephone rings

Cue 2   **Body:** "Mother of God!"   (Page 11)
         Clap of thunder

Cue 3   **Body:** "… 'No room at the Inn'."   (Page 11)
         Dull rumble of thunder

Cue 4   Short, loud scream, off   (Page 14)
         Crash of thunder

MADE AND PRINTED IN GREAT BRITAIN BY
LATIMER TREND & COMPANY LTD PLYMOUTH

MADE IN ENGLAND